The
CONCLUSION
TRAP

Four Steps To Better Decisions

D & L Publications
Corte Madera, CA

www.theconclusiontrap.com

For Lynn, the best foxhole buddy in the world.

Acknowledgements

My name may be the only one on the cover, but no book is truly the product of a single individual. *The Conclusion Trap* wouldn't exist without the help of friends and colleagues.

Rich Sheridan and Beth Polish are the spiritual parents of the book. Rich provided the original story that so astonished me I had to tell everyone about it, and Beth, with her pretzel croissants and half-caffeinated coffee, saw the path to turn it into something much larger.

Roger Chen, Jeff Fuchs, Paul Lewis, and Kevin Meyer bolstered the narrative with stories adding depth and color.

Michael Brody, Anne Covey, Mark Graban, Josh Groves, Rob Kaufman, and Chris Lynch found the logical flaws, confusing points, and sloppy writing that eluded me.

Brent Wahba gets credit for the best metaphor in the book (the "crime scene"), as well as the title.

Sally Dominguez, Arin Fishkin, and Imogen Speer's graphic genius turned my words into images and pictures that are worth well more than a thousand words.

And Tom Ehrenfeld, as always, was beside me the whole way with his inevitably insightful (albeit sometimes infuriating) criticism and suggestions. Stepping out of one's comfort zone is considerably less scary when you have an editor like Tom by your side.

Thank you all.

Contents

PART 1:
THE MANIFESTO

AS A MANAGEMENT CONSULTANT, I've seen more than my fair share of ludicrous corporate decisions resulting from hasty leaps to poorly designed solutions. The good news for me is that they often lead to business when companies must reckon with the consequences, and they need help figuring out what their real problems are and how to fix them.

Before becoming a consultant, though, I was an employee at several companies over the course of 15 years, and I've lived through the ramifications of these poor decisions. I've seen the sales declines, the layoffs, and the damaged lives. Heck, I've been laid off myself, and have spent my fair share of time at the unemployment office.

Frankly, I'm tired.

Tired of seeing leaders jump to conclusions and taking action without really understanding their problem.

Tired of seeing leaders arrive at a "solution" that doesn't solve the real problem at all.

Tired of seeing the staggering waste of money and opportunity caused by this knee-jerk approach to problem solving.

Of course, truly understanding a problem is no guarantee that (1) you'll make the right decision, and that (2) the decision will pay off. But it's the smart way to bet. While it's often said that it's better to be lucky than good, that's not a great strategy for success.

I want to help you succeed by making better decisions.

So in this manifesto, I'll present a clear and simple approach that will give you the skills and confidence to find, frame, and attack the root causes of your problems, and thereby reduce the likelihood that you'll jump to the wrong conclusion.

THE ROADMAP

First, I'll show you how to spot the signs of conclusion jumping.

Second, I'll explain the root causes of conclusion jumping.

Third, I'll teach you a process that will keep you from conclusion jumping.

STORY #1
YEAH, BUT I WANT AN APP!

My friend Rich runs a custom software company. One day last year, the president of a nationwide firm asked him to design a smartphone app. The nationwide firm had grown by acquiring smaller companies around the country, but even though they were now part of the same organization, they weren't passing sales leads from one region to another.

Rich wanted to talk to the potential users in the regional offices to better understand their needs. But the president didn't want to waste time on that research—he just knew that an app would fix the problem by making it easier to share leads.

Rich insisted on doing the research. Staff in multiple regional offices told him they would never use a smartphone app to pass leads to another region. Their bonus system was structured such that they'd be penalized for passing a lead to a different region.

After talking with many employees, Rich told the president that the problem was the compensation structure, not the technology. He pointed out that if the regional salespeople had the right incentives, they would use telephones, or faxes, or carrier pigeons, or whatever they needed to in order to hand off the lead.

The president of the company said, "That's fine, but I still want an app."

As you might guess, Rich's company didn't get the business. I'm not sure whether or not the president eventually got his app from

another company. But you already know how the story ends—
wasting time and money on technology that no one used.

STORY #2
THE REORGANIZATION FALLACY

Years ago, I worked at Asics, the sporting goods company. After
several consecutive years of strong growth, sales had gone into a
tailspin. Up to that point, the media was calling Asics a sleeping
giant about to shake up the industry. But apparently it was
actually going into a coma.

Take a highly competitive CEO and place under high pressure
to reverse a sales decline. What do you get? One of the classic
responses to falling sales: reorganization.

The CEO broke up the single footwear division into multiple
business units—running, cross-training, basketball, tennis,
wrestling, kids, etc. Everyone moved offices. Everyone got new
business cards.

Unfortunately, Asics didn't have all the right people and
necessary skills to staff the new organization. And even if it had,
it wouldn't have mattered. The company's main issues had to do
with product design and product pricing. The seats people sat in
had nothing to do with the real problems.

The result? After a few months, everyone ended up doing pretty
much the same work as they had before. Within six months Asics laid
off 20% of the employees. Immediately after that, the president was
fired. And within 18 months, the company reorganized again right
back to where it started.

STORY #3
MORE IS BETTER, RIGHT?

My friend Kevin was running the largest molding facility of a medical device manufacturer in the mid-1990s, making components for disposable drug infusion pump cassettes.

The plant had 60 heavy presses running non-stop, but they were falling further and further behind customer demand. When Kevin transferred into the job, they were about three months behind in meeting production, which meant that they were starving their downstream factories of raw materials and forcing them to shut down.

The corporate office was not happy. Especially since the answer was obvious: If you're running production 24/7/365 and you can't keep up with demand, you clearly need more machines.

So corporate bought a bunch more presses. Two million dollars worth. Unfortunately, the machines had a six-month lead time, so Kevin had to figure out something in the short term to get the top brass off his back.

He studied lean manufacturing principles and learned how to speed up the changeover of machines. Machines have to be shut down when you want to change the molds, and that downtime cuts into production time. Faster changeover means less downtime, which means more production for the downstream factories.

Similarly, he realized that they needed to shut down presses for maintenance so that they could run at a high level with fewer defects. He switched to shorter production runs with more frequent maintenance, which led to improved quality and fewer defects.

The result of his efforts was a dramatic increase in production. By the time the new presses came in six months later, they had almost caught up to demand.

Too bad about the $2 million in machines they didn't need anymore.

MILO, TOCK, AND THE HUMBUG

In *The Phantom Tollbooth*, Norton Juster's fabulous children's book, Milo, Tock, and the Humbug literally jump to (the Isle of) Conclusions. It doesn't take much—in Milo's case, it was just a comment on what a nice day it was for a drive.

> *"It certainly couldn't be a nicer day," agreed Milo, who was too busy looking at the road to see that the others had gone. And in a split second he was gone also.*

> *He landed next to Tock and the terrified Humbug on the tiny island, which now looked completely different. Instead of palms and flowers, there were only rocks and the twisted stumps of long-dead trees. It certainly didn't seem like the same place they had seen from the road.*

In Juster's imagination, the Isle of Conclusions is a nasty place— it looks much better from afar—and distressingly easy to get to. As a character in the book tells Milo,

> *It's really quite simple: every time you decide something without having a good reason, you jump to Conclusions whether you like it or not. It's such an easy trip to make that I've been here hundreds of times.*

And this is the situation that the three companies I've described found themselves in. The conclusions they jumped to—a smartphone app; a reorganization; a bunch of expensive machinery—looked attractive from a distance, but the reality wasn't nearly as effective or as profitable as they thought.

In *The Phantom Tollbooth*, Milo learns that, sadly, you can't escape the Isle of Conclusions as easily as you got there. There's only one way off the island—with a long, hard swim in the "Sea of Knowledge," which is another perfect metaphor for the journey that leaders have to go through.

NO CRYSTAL BALLS

Everyone makes bad decisions sometimes. When you have imperfect information—and trying to predict the future in your business means that by definition you have imperfect information—you're going to guess wrong sometimes. Sadly, no one has a crystal ball.

Wrong decisions are okay. Wrong decisions are the price of doing business. Of being human.

What's not okay are rash decisions based on an insufficient effort to understand the real problem. What's not okay is jumping to conclusions and implementing "solutions" that jeopardize your organization and the lives of the people that work there. What's not okay is the undisciplined or non-existent analysis visible in the "Ready, fire, aim!" habit that so many leaders have.

This book is not an attack on wrong decisions, or results that happen to turn out badly. It's an attack on the second kind of error—rash decisions based on jumping to conclusions.

CLASSIC SIGNS OF TROUBLE

When you don't understand the real problem and simply jump to a conclusion, you tend to reach for one of three solutions:

1. Shiny new technology
2. Reorganization
3. Money

Of course, there are other knee-jerk solutions, but if one of these is your answer to a problem—stop.

Think again.

You may actually be right. You might really need to develop new tech, or create a new organizational structure, or spend more money. But more often than not, you're about to go down the wrong road. You'll have a shinier, more expensive, differently organized version of the same problem that you had before.

Except that you'll be two months or two years farther down the road, and farther behind your competitors.

CONCLUSIONS ⇨ SOLUTIONS

In daily life, we talk about jumping to conclusions. But in an environment where you have to take some sort of action—for example, in a business or medical setting—you can just as easily say jumping to **solutions**.

After all, the purpose of reaching a conclusion is to devise a solution so that you can move forward.

Unfortunately, when you jump to an incorrect conclusion, your solution is almost inevitably wrong.

In other words, what at first appears to be the solution, isn't.

... AND WHAT APPEARS TO BE THE PROBLEM, ISN'T

The company in my first story went for shiny new technology. Why not? Smartphone apps are all the rage. People love smartphone apps. All the cool companies have smartphone apps. If you've got a problem, surely an app will solve it.

To be fair to the president of that company, the existing systems for referrals and lead transfers *were* clunky. The company had been cobbled together from smaller firms around the country, and they lacked an easy way to share important information. Salespeople (especially when they work on commission) are busy. And they're not reluctant to complain about poorly designed systems (especially when they work on commission).

But as Rich discovered, lousy technology wasn't the problem. The real problem was the compensation system. No amount of shiny new tech would address that.

FIXES THAT FAIL

I survived four reorganizations during my time working in corporate America. They all looked good on paper. None of them made a difference to our bottom lines.

In my second story, the president at Asics hoped that reorganization would improve sales. Clearly, it didn't work out that way. The reorg didn't address the real problems with our products and pricing.

Moreover, like most reorganizations, it destroyed the relationships, experience, and tribal knowledge that expedite decision-making and improve performance. Reorganizations bulldoze those intangible assets into oblivion, ensuring that for six months at least, a company will be operating much less effectively.

People who study system dynamics refer to "fixes that fail." Fixes that fail either create unintended—and problematic—consequences, or they exacerbate the original problem. For example, a company that wants to cut costs might choose to reduce maintenance on their machines. In the short term, costs do go down—the company saves money on labor, supplies, and replacement parts. But over the long run, machines begin to break down more frequently, product quality declines, and total costs eventually increase.

Cities dealing with traffic congestion implement a classic fix that fails: they build more roads to increase capacity. Unfortunately, less congested roads encourage more people to drive, eventually leading to even more traffic than before. (A better fix would be to improve mass transit, or to change zoning laws to allow commercial and residential buildings to be built in the same place and reduce the need for so much driving.)

More often than not, reorganizations are a fix that fails.

Why? Because customers have zero interest in how you're organized internally. They want good products and services at fair prices. If they're not buying from you, the problem is almost certainly not related to the fact that you have a VP of Sales, and not a "Brand Warrior," a Customer Service Director instead of a "Chief Happiness Officer," or a head of research instead of a "Galactic Viceroy of Research Excellence." (All of which are real titles, by the way.)

Changing people's seats has about as much chance of improving your situation as changing the Weather Channel has of improving your actual weather. 99.9% of the time, the root cause of your problems is not the org chart.

If your customers aren't buying, you need to look at more fundamental elements of your company than the title on people's business cards.

Does the product meet customer needs—or even better, exceed them?

Is your service competitive?

Is the price right?

PART II:
WE HAVE
MET THE
ENEMY AND
HE IS US

"WE HAVE MET THE ENEMY AND HE IS US" (a twist on Commodore Oliver Hazard Perry's boast after defeating the British at Lake Erie) was cartoonist Walt Kelly's way of pointing out how the United States undermined its own efforts in the Vietnam War. The same can be said of our own efforts to deal with the problems we're facing: our cognitive biases and our training make us our own worst enemy.

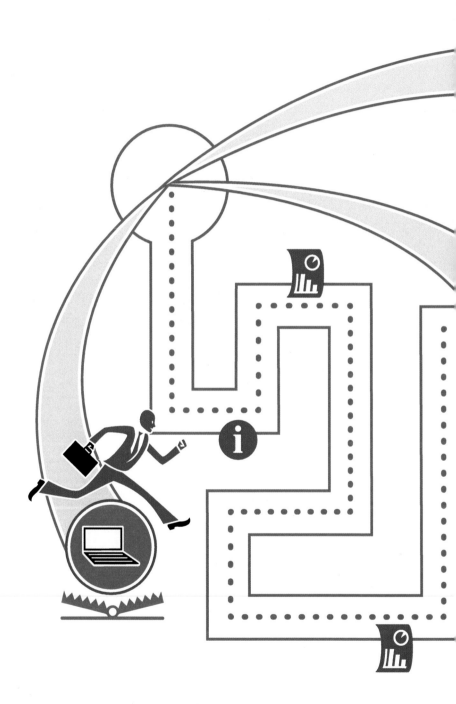

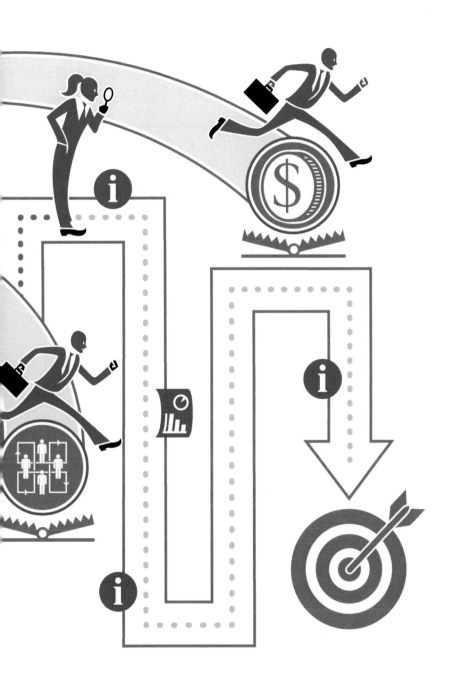

THE JUMPER AND THE ANALYST

It's natural that we jump to conclusions and come up with half-baked "solutions." We're wired that way.

Don't beat yourself up. It's an unavoidable aspect of the human condition.

In his book *Thinking, Fast and Slow*, Daniel Kahneman describes two different modes of thinking that we use when experiencing the world.

System 1 (or "fast" thinking) operates most of the time. It's our brain's automatic, intuitive approach to dealing with the external world. It's what enables us to make nearly instantaneous judgments about what we see without having to think too hard. System 1 is what causes you to jump backwards when you hear a rattlesnake's tail. It's what enables you to complete the phrase "peanut butter and..." It's what you use when you solve "2+2=?" It's what makes you associate "Rolls-Royce" with luxury.

System 1 is essentially unconscious. It's also essentially unstoppable. Just try **not** solving "2+2=?" Or try **not** jumping away from the rattlesnake.

System 2 ("slow" thinking) is the opposite. It's effortful, logical, conscious, and energy intensive. You use System 2 when you solve "14 x 24." You use it when you're trying to figure out which healthcare plan to select during open enrollment at your company, or how to manage multiple transfers in the Tokyo subway system.

System 1 and System 2 is hard to remember. Let's call them "Jumping" and "Analyzing," or the Jumper and the Analyst.

YOU ONLY THINK YOU'RE AN ANALYST.

We identify with the Analyst. It feels like who we "really" are—the careful thinker, the rational leader, the prudent decider.

But really, you're not. You'd be miserable and overwhelmed if you were an Analyst all the time—at least, you would be if you weren't bitten by the rattlesnake first.

Most of the time, you're a Jumper. The Analyst is on standby in the background. It kicks in when the Jumper runs into trouble and you need the big cognitive guns to handle the situation.

This division of labor makes life considerably easier than it would be if you operated as an Analyst all the time. Depending on the context, the ability to Jump is not only useful, it can actually be lifesaving (as when you hear a rattlesnake). But defaulting to Jumping creates all kinds of problems. It leads you to conclusions when you should actually be carefully gathering data, weighing evidence, considering options, and only then arriving at a solution.

KNEE-JERKS

How does the Jumper read this?

~~JUMPING TO CONCLUSIONS~~

JUMPING TO CONCLUSIONS, right?

Wrong.

If you had activated your internal Analyst (But why would you? This question is a no brainer.), you might have considered how letters are shaped, and what other letters might be under the black bar. Like this:

IUMRING TQ GQNGIUSIQNS

Jumping is great. Except when it's not.

WE'RE OBLIVIOUS

Our tendency to jump to conclusions is so deeply wired in our brains that we're not even aware we're doing it.

Think of the last time someone cut you off in traffic. How did you react? What did you think?

(Pause here while you think about it.)

You probably thought that it was obnoxious at best and dangerous at worst—and your internal Jumper came to the conclusion that the driver was either a jerk (at best) or an automotive menace (at worst). In fact, it feels good to jump to that conclusion. You get to work yourself into righteous anger. You've been wronged! How dare that lousy so-and-so cut you off in traffic!

This is the fundamental attribution error at work. You've jumped to the conclusion that the lousy driving was due to the other driver's personal character, rather than to external factors.

However, the Analyst would ask *why* the other driver cut you off. Maybe her dog got hit by a bicycle, was bleeding and whimpering on the seat, and she was rushing her pet to the vet. Maybe he was on the way to the airport to meet his wife coming back from a deployment in Afghanistan. You'd probably be less concerned with road etiquette in those situations—and you'd be more forgiving as well.

Or picture this scenario: you're in a long line at the airport newsstand trying to buy a bottle of water. There are two cash registers and two people working at the newsstand, but only one is at a register. The other one is restocking the refrigerator and the candy shelves. What do you think? What conclusion do you jump to?

Did you blame the person restocking the refrigerator for being completely oblivious to the long line of customers?

Or did you conclude that the store's management has a terrible process for checking people out? I mean, it's obvious: when you have a long line of people, workers should staff both registers, right?

(Before you go on, pause. Reflect. What else could be going on? What other reasons might there be for the long line, other than lousy employees?)

Stop your internal Jumper, and ask *why* they weren't staffing both registers.

Maybe the other register is broken. Maybe the person restocking shelves is a temp and hadn't been trained to use the register. Or maybe the workers hadn't been trained that when the customer line gets over four people, they should quit stocking shelves and open both registers.

The second of the Buddha's Four Noble Truths states that the root of suffering is attachment. Everything in the world is transient, so it's wise not to get attached to anything or the way anything currently is.

The Buddha wasn't talking about conclusions, but the wisdom holds: don't be attached to your initial conclusion. Suspend judgment for a few moments and give yourself time to think more deeply about the situation in front of you.

That will give the Analyst time to think.

YEAH, BUT I WANT AN APP! (REDUX)

Think about the company president in my first story who was absolutely convinced that he needed an app. This is an outstanding example of Jumping at work:

Salespeople don't pass along leads.

➥ Our CRM software stinks.

    ➥ Conclusion: salespeople don't pass along leads *because* the software stinks.

        ➥ Solution: we need better software—and an app is the answer.

The logic proceeds as inexorably as "peanut butter and...."

Asking *why* leads aren't shared requires activating the Analyst. Otherwise, we just jump to conclusions. Analyzing is hard work. It's energy intensive. It's time consuming. And when the Jumper is running the cognitive show, it seems utterly unnecessary.

Of course the Jumper knows the answer. We need an app.

Or, in other words, IUMRING TQ GQNGIUSIQNS.

LOST IN THE FOG

Recently, a major European bank was struggling with low profitability. The leadership team decided that the route to higher profitability was to get more business from high net worth individuals who could deposit $100 million or more with them.

Of course, getting people to invest that kind of money isn't trivial.

Let's Jump along with the leadership team:

We don't have enough clients who want to deposit $100 million.

➡ We don't have a special group to handle those clients.

    ➡ Conclusion: we don't have those clients **because** we don't have a special group.

        ➡ Solution: if we form a group, we'll get the business (i.e., "If you build it, they will come.").

The leadership team reorganized and created a special "Family Office Group" (FOG) to cater to those clients' needs. And they waited for the money to roll in.

For nine months. After which time, with no new clients, they closed down the FOG group.

The real problem, of course, wasn't the lack of a special team with a goofy acronym. The real problem is that there just aren't that many people who are able to give $100 million to a bank to manage. And those that are rich enough typically have a family office of their own to manage their money, or they give it to Goldman Sachs, which has more cachet in that very small market.

In the meantime, the leadership team starved the groups that managed less wealthy clients of resources: experts in tax law and estate planning weren't available to help teams that catered to those customers, and new, talented hires went into the FOG. The user-facing technology (website, online banking, etc.), which was easily three years behind its competitors and frustrating for customers, didn't get a much-needed upgrade.

It was an expensive jump to the Isle of Conclusions.

WHERE IMPORTANT WORK GOES TO DIE

Several years ago, I did a small consulting project at an outdoor goods company. It was taking the customer service department between four and seven days to approve a customer (i.e., retailer) credit request. Retailers wanted a faster response.

Here's how the system worked: a customer would call the rep and request a credit. The rep would fill out a paper form and walk it over to the customer service manager for approval. The manager would review the request, approve it, and return the form to the rep so that it could be processed.

The manager thought the problem was the paper form that the customer service rep used to log the claim. I mean, who uses paper forms for that kind of request—especially when the company had a solid CRM software system?

For the manager, the solution was obvious. (Warning: Jumping ahead!):

It takes seven days to process a customer credit.

➡ We use paper credit forms.

   ➡ Conclusion: it takes us seven days to process the credit *because* we use paper.

      ➡ Solution: develop a web-based or electronic form and get rid of the paper.

Of course, it would take 3-4 weeks to design the form and integrate it into the CRM system, but the problem would be solved.

Or not. It turns out the big delay in issuing the credit memo was waiting for the customer service manager to review the request. The paper could sit in his inbox for up to a full week before he looked at it. The rest of the process was actually very fast.

If they had an electronic form, it would have sat in his *email inbox* for up to a full week. And nothing would have changed.

AT LEAST IT WASN'T SHAG CARPETING

In his book *Lean Hospitals*, author Mark Graban tells a classic story of jumping to solutions. At a U.S. hospital a few years ago, patient surveys showed that late-night noise was the biggest cause of complaints. Those complaints lowered patient satisfaction scores, which are very important to the CEO and the board.

The CEO decided that carpeting in the hallways would reduce the noise. Here's the Jumper at work:

Late night noise is a problem for patients.

➡ Linoleum hallways are noisy.

  ➡ Carpeting absorbs noise.

    ➡ Conclusion: our hallways are noisy *because* they don't have carpeting.

     ➡ Solution: install carpeting so that hallways and patient rooms will be quieter.

The hospital spent a fair bit of money buying and installing the carpeting. Oddly, patient satisfaction data showed that noise complaints dropped starting the month before the carpet was installed.

Why? While the leadership team was Jumping to solutions, the nurses activated their inner Analysts and discovered that TVs were a major source of ambient noise. As the carpeting was being sourced, purchased, and installed, they took the initiative to make small improvements, such as closing doors and turning TV volumes down at night.

In an elegantly ironic example of a fix that failed, the previous year the CEO had decided that nurses should spend more time at patient bedsides. The hospital purchased mobile computers to allow nurses to move away from their station. But the new carpet made it physically harder for nurses to push computer carts down those hallways—so they ended up spending more time at the nurses' station.

WHO GETS THE GOLD STAR?

We jump to solutions because, for the most part, it makes daily life easier.

But we're also products of our environment. In a Pavlovian sense (stimulus-response), we're trained for that kind of thinking.

Think back to grade school. The teacher asks a question. Who gets picked to answer it?

The kid who had his or her hand up first.

Sure, good teachers try not to always pick the fastest kid, but they call on the first hand a disproportionate amount of the time. So the fast kids get gold stars and great class participation grades.

If you're a bit slower, or more thoughtful, or don't fully understand the question? No gold star for you.

This trend repeats in high school. And college. And beyond. I went to Stanford Business School—same thing. In school at any level, it's better to be quick than thoughtful. So when you finally get into the corporate world, you've been trained to be fast with an answer.

Which is a good thing. Because if you want a good annual review and a promotion, you try to be the person about whom the boss says, "Sarah is amazing. In meetings she always seems to have an answer for our sticky problems. She's fast with a plan, and faster to implement."

You do not want to be the person who says, "I'm not sure I really understand the problem. I think we should spend more time gathering facts and data to make sure we really know what's going on."

Business moves faster than ever. No one wants to hear that you want more time. No one gets a gold star for slowing down the train—even if the train is speeding towards disaster.

TOO BUSY?

If I had an hour to solve a problem, I'd spend 55 minutes thinking about the problem and five minutes thinking about solutions.

—Albert Einstein

This quote, often attributed to Einstein, points us to the second primary cause of leaping to solutions: people are too busy to spend enough time thinking about the problem.

We immediately jump to conclusions because it's fast and easy. But it doesn't explain why we don't take the time to analyze a situation thoroughly.

That answer is prosaic. We're really busy at work.

Research from Babson College and Wharton indicates that we spend nearly 80% of our workday responding to emails, in meetings, or on the phone.[1] That leaves precious little time for deep thinking about one's own work. And as companies expand their global presence, there's an excellent chance that we're dealing with colleagues in multiple time zones, lengthening the workday and adding to our workload.

Not only that, but email and other forms of electronic communication (Slack, text messages, etc.) have exacerbated the problem. Because we can send messages instantaneously, we've come to expect instant responses from others—and we assume that others are expecting an instant response from us as well. Modern communication tools, and the organizational norms around them, have encouraged the Jumper over the Analyst.

SPENDING MONEY INSTEAD OF TIME

Who wants to spend the time to really investigate a problem? It's practically self-preservation to skip the investigation in favor of grasping at the easy and obvious answer.

That's what happened at the second company I wrote about earlier. How long would it take to understand that the real problem wasn't a lack of machines, but a lack of machine capacity? And how long would it take to learn how to increase capacity without buying new presses?

Studying the art of quick machine changeover is time consuming. Kevin spent weeks learning how to do it and teaching his team on the shop floor. Analyzing the correlation of maintenance frequency on defect rates also takes time. And when top management is breathing down your neck to increase output, that's the last thing you want to do.

---

1   Rob Cross, Rob Rebele, and Adam Grant, "Collaborative Overload," *Harvard Business Review*, January-February 2016.

It's a lot easier to just buy $2 million worth of new presses so you can move onto the next problem.

Now you might think, "Hey—new presses would have increased production too!" And you're right. But I'd venture that you'd prefer to have higher output without the $2 million-dollar price tag.

PROCESSES. NOT BAND-AIDS.

Martin Memorial Health System in Florida almost spent $300,000 on new IV pumps because they were too busy to fully understand the problem they were facing.

The nursing staff spent about 40 minutes per shift looking for IV pumps. Naturally, they thought that they didn't have enough pumps, and that they needed to order more. Conclusion jumping at its finest.

But upon further investigation, the hospital discovered that in fact it had 508 pumps to serve 344 beds. Based on the national IV pump-to-bed ratio of 1.2 pumps per bed, they actually had 96 more pumps than the typical hospital of the same size.

They came to realize that the real problem was not a shortage of pumps. It was the absence of an efficient system for nurses to access pumps quickly and easily. This lack led nurses to hoard unused pumps so that they could find pumps more quickly when they wanted them—and that made the problem even worse for the hospital as a whole.

It takes time to create new procedures and processes. It's much faster to buy new IV pumps—and even if that wouldn't solve the underlying problem, it would mask the symptoms.

To the hospital's credit, it took the time to understand and solve the real problem. It installed "equipment supermarkets" in nursing units that contained all the necessary equipment for that unit, and created standard procedures to increase the availability of needed equipment. The equipment supermarket shelving was color coded and numbered with the quantity of items for each color: green (supply is adequate); yellow (supply needs replenishing); and red (need for immediate restocking).

This solution reduced nursing time spent gathering equipment to less than one minute per shift. By improving the use of IV pumps, the hospital was able to replace the existing pump inventory with 100 fewer units, yielding savings of $300,000.[2]

THE RFID KILLER

Roger Chen was the head of continuous improvement at a health system in Florida. They nicknamed him the RFID Killer.

Roger joined the hospital when it was getting ready to spend $600,000 on a radio frequency identification system (RFID) to track equipment. As at Martin Memorial, nurses could never find the equipment they needed quickly and easily.

Roger put a stop to that. He took the time to turn on his inner Analyst, seeking to fully understand the problem first, before trying to solve it. His team mapped the flow of equipment throughout the hospital. Although there were differences in specifics from the Martin Memorial situation, he was able to implement many of the same countermeasures. He created supermarkets and appropriate processes to ensure that none of

---

2   Information in this story comes from John Toussaint and Leonard Berry, "The Promise of Lean in Healthcare", **Mayo Clinic Proceedings**, January 2013, Volume 88, Issue 1, pp.74-82.

the equipment got lost within the building, and nurses didn't feel the need to create a private stash. No RFID needed.

Jumping to conclusions—and solutions—is fast. Understanding the real problem takes time, which often seems impossible to find in a world where people handle work emails at 11pm. But isn't it worth a bit of time to save $600,000?

WHO'S REALLY THE PROBLEM?

Finding the real problem often requires you to look in the mirror. Sometimes the root cause of a problem is you.

It's easy to blame others—suppliers, customers, employees, equipment, regulators, etc. Looking in the mirror isn't always pleasant.

Reckoning with absurd policies and hasty decisions we've made that cause people real pain isn't a lot of fun.

An unwillingness to look in the mirror and see our own complicity in the problem leads to the third reason we so often turn to the Jumper instead of the Analyst. Who wants to acknowledge that we're the ones who have screwed up?

ADAPTING TO ABSURDITY

The CEO of a plastic extrusion company in Maryland complained that his employees in the purchasing department were "undisciplined" because they weren't adhering to a process that he had set up earlier.

"We have a perfect procurement process, but employees don't follow it," he said.

Here's how the company's "perfect process" worked: All purchase requests, no matter how trivial, needed to go through the VP of Operations. Need more pens, Post-It notes, or paper clips? Get the VP's signature. To make matters worse, all requests over $250 went up another level and had to be approved by the CFO.

The simplest purchase approval took three weeks. If you had an emergency request—for example, a replacement part for the air conditioning system—you'd have been out of luck if you followed the process. So the "undisciplined" employees created workarounds to get the things they needed more quickly and easily.

The CEO and CFO originally installed these human checks (i.e., the approval by the VP and CFO) in an effort to increase visibility into expenditures and control costs. They didn't understand the real problem—that the company lacked a thoughtfully designed process to ensure that purchases were appropriate. Their solution—a fix that failed—made the situation even worse.

The lack of discipline wasn't due to lazy, headstrong workers. It was necessary adaptation to foolish policies designed by the company leadership.

But understanding the real problem, of course, requires looking in the mirror. In an increasingly competitive, global market, honest self-reflection and candor is critical. The fault, as Shakespeare wrote, often lies not in our stars, but in ourselves.

FLUSHING $90 BILLION DOWN THE TOILET

In the 1980s, Roger Smith, then-CEO of General Motors, spent $90 billion on new plants and equipment—including a massive number of robots for auto assembly. It's not clear exactly how much of that money was spent on the robots themselves, but it's safe to say that it was in the billions of dollars.

(It's worth pointing out that although this story is 30 years old, the lessons are still relevant today. Just because something happened a while ago doesn't mitigate the lessons—just ask economists or Wall Street traders about the Dutch tulip bubble.)

By the mid-80s, GM (and the other Detroit automakers) were being destroyed by Toyota, Honda, and Nissan. GM couldn't make the small cars that Americans wanted to buy at a profit. And it certainly couldn't match the Japanese cars' quality.

Smith decided that the problem was clearly the workers—after all, its unionized United Auto Worker employees had high hourly wages, and they were the ones that made lousy cars. With that assumption as a starting point, the answer was obvious: build a "lights out" factory—entirely run by robots, with no people needed. Sure, there'd be higher startup expenses, but lower costs in the long run. And with the finest robots and software controlling them, there'd be no quality problems.

It didn't quite work out that way.

The apotheosis—and the nadir—of this technological fantasy was the GM factory in Hamtramck, MI. None of the technology worked the way they hoped. The hundreds of robots should have reduced the number of autoworkers needed. But the factory still had 5,000 workers on payroll, as much as a regular auto plant, to deal with various quality issues and production problems. There was no chance Smith's plan was going to work with 1980s technology. In fact, it doesn't even work now with technology 30 years more advanced: In 2016, Elon Musk admitted that "excessive automation [for the Tesla Model 3 assembly line] ... was a mistake" and that "humans are underrated." His plant was insanely expensive, inflexible, and incapable of producing top quality cars. There are just too many problems, and too many variables, to completely eliminate the need for human ingenuity and judgment in car production.

In any event, Roger Smith didn't want to look in the mirror. It's much easier to blame someone else for problems of your own creation.

But if he had looked in the mirror, he would have seen his own fingerprints on GM's quality problems. He would have recognized the spectacular, cringe-worthy irony in announcing a new management compensation formula that made it easier for all the executives (including him) to earn bonuses—on the very same day that the UAW approved wage concessions to save money. That's a move guaranteed to undermine labor-management relations.

He would have seen plant managers telling workers to skip quality checks, eliminate planned tool changes, and ignore machining processes that were clearly deteriorating. That's obviously not a recipe for producing the high-quality cars that customers wanted, and were buying from the Japanese companies—but when the performance evaluation system you've designed prioritizes meeting production quotas at all costs, well, you can understand why the plant managers kept the lines running. Never mind what that meant for quality.

He would have seen the separate bathrooms at the Tonawanda, NY engine plant—one for hourly workers, and one for management—which undermined the cohesion that's essential in forging a strong team with a shared goal.

GM's problem wasn't the workers. It was the managers. Or more accurately, it was the management system set up by Smith and other executives.

When GM eventually started a joint venture with Toyota in Fremont, CA, the plant went from GM's worst in quality to best in just one year—with all the same front-line employees. The only thing that changed was the adoption of the Toyota management system. Dozens of books have been written on this system, but one of the core tenets is a nearly religious avoidance of solution jumping, coupled with a structured approach to root cause problem solving.

You can spend $90 billion, but unless you look in the mirror and activate your inner Analyst first, you probably won't solve the real problem.

4 STEPS TO BETTER DECISIONS

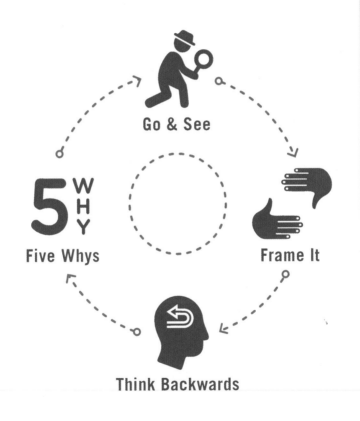

Go & See

Frame It

Think Backwards

Five Whys

PART III: PREVENTATIVE MEASURES

YOU'LL NEVER GET PAST THE TENDENCY TO LEAP TO SOLUTIONS. But there are ways to fight that tendency, to promote deep analytical thinking instead of Jumping. Here's a four-step process to help you activate your inner Analyst and keep you from jumping to ill-informed solutions.

GO AND SEE

*A desk is a dangerous place from
which to view the world.*
—John le Carré

IT'S EASY TO JUMP TO CONCLUSIONS and lousy
solutions—when you don't have a clear picture of what's
actually happening.

And you can't have a clear picture if you don't leave your desk,
your office, or your conference room.

Unfortunately, that's where most leaders live.

Taiichi Ohno was the father of the Toyota Production System, or what is now known as "lean." As described in *The Birth of Lean*,

> *[Ohno] never rendered judgment simply on the basis of hearing about something. He always insisted on going to the place in question and having a look.*

(I mention Toyota because it's arguably the greatest manufacturing success story of the last 75 years. From near bankruptcy following WWII, the company has become the most profitable automaker in the world. It's number two in size behind the Volkswagen group of brands, and—get this—hasn't laid off workers due to slow demand since 1950. It's true that the company did close its plant in Australia, but the entire auto industry, including key suppliers, pulled out of the country because it's too small to support domestic auto manufacturing.)

Ohno said, "Data is of course important in manufacturing, but I place the greatest emphasis on facts." You can leave out the word "manufacturing," and apply the concept to anything in your company or your life. Facts are more important than data.

When he talked about his preference for facts over data, he was urging people to go and see for themselves. Gathering facts comes from close observation of people, of objects, of spaces.

By contrast, spreadsheets, reports, and anecdotal accounts are not facts. They're data. They're two-dimensional representations of reality, which makes it easy to jump to conclusions.

Data tells you how often a machine breaks down on an assembly line. Facts—direct observation—show you that the machine is dirty, covered in oil, and hasn't been cleaned and maintained in a long time.

Data tells you that customers applying for a mortgage forget to fill out certain parts of forms, forcing bank employees to follow up with customers and delaying the underwriting process. Facts—close examination of the form, and direct observation of an applicant while filling out the forms—reveal that one of the forms is poorly laid out and so cluttered that it's easy to overlook a box.

Data tells you that the employee attrition rate is higher than industry average. Facts—spending a day in the office where people work—show that the office is kind of dark and unpleasant, that there's no space for quiet reflection, and that the company you outsource facility services to doesn't do a good job of cleaning the bathrooms.

BOTH FACTS AND DATA

Data without facts gives you an anemic, two-dimensional, black and white view of the world. Facts without data give you color and texture, but not the detailed insight you'll need to solve the thorniest problems.

Facts will tell you to clean and maintain the machines on the assembly line, but data will help you figure out how often you need to do it to ensure quality.

Facts will tell you that you need to improve the layout of the mortgage application forms, but data will tell you what the new error rate is, and by how much you've improved the materials.

You need both facts and data.

THE CRIME SCENE

Where do you go to get the facts? The same place that any self-respecting detective goes on a cop show. You go to the crime scene.

Obviously, we're not dealing with murders or robberies here. The "crime scene" in this case is where the work gets done, and where the problems occur.

It's where the IT department writes code for your company's software. It's the bank teller's desk where customers open accounts. It's the warehouse where your box is picked, packed, and shipped. It's the kitchen where you cook dinner.

Going to the scene of the crime means avoiding the temptation to sequester yourself in your office or conference room. It means that you can observe what's happening firsthand, ask questions of the people working there, and learn what the facts really are.

The president of the company who wanted an app to increase lead sharing clearly didn't go to the crime scene, where the regional salespeople worked. If he had, he would have learned that the problem wasn't the technology, but the bonus system. Rich's software team, who went to the those offices, figured it out pretty quickly.

LOUSY WORKERS OR LOUSY SYSTEMS?

You can't understand a problem when you only see data. Nothing substitutes for direct observation.

Early in my career when I worked at Asics, we struggled with shipping errors. The reports from the IT department showed that our customer service team was making mistakes when they entered orders.

Looking only at the data would lead you to believe that the customer service reps were either (1) lazy; (2) incompetent; or (3) poorly trained.

But they weren't. We sat and watched the customer service reps for an hour while they did their work. We found poorly designed order entry screens that made it easy for them to make errors when keying in orders.

If we had jumped to solutions, we would have either hired new reps who were "better," or we would have put everyone through another training program. Instead, we redesigned the order entry screens and kept all of our dedicated, experienced reps.

Problem solved.

DON'T BE A STRANGER

CBS's reality TV show, *Undercover Boss*, provides viewers with the thrill of *schadenfreude*. We get to see a highly paid CEO receive his comeuppance as he experiences first-hand the dirty, difficult, dangerous, or demoralizing reality of many of the jobs in the company.

We snicker at the clueless CEO who didn't know that the air conditioner in the warehouse (in Alabama, in the summer) has been broken for three weeks because of his order to cut expenses; that it takes four levels of approval to order more paper for the copy machine; that demands to increase productivity mean that there's no time to go to the bathroom.

And of course, no one recognizes that the new guy driving the truck or loading the boxes is the CEO.

The first sign that you don't go and see often enough? The workers don't recognize you.

YOU'RE NOT A KING VISITING THE SERFS

Many executives think they're going to the crime scene to learn the facts. In actuality, they're more like a king visiting the serfs.

A leading global financial services company that boasts of its focus on customer service requires executives to visit its call centers so that they can see the customer interactions first-hand. That sounds good in concept, but it doesn't really work that way. The executives leave their marble-floored, mahogany-lined offices in NY, take the corporate jet to the inexpensive, second-tier locations around the world, and sit through a series of PowerPoint presentations. Then they listen in on a few calls with the best customer service rep, write an obligatory "lessons learned" email, and fly back in time to make dinner in Manhattan.

This is not visiting the crime scene.

Visiting the crime scene is: the former credit card company MBNA rquiring all executives to spend four hours a month listening to customer calls. Not only that, they were forbidden to have unlisted home phone numbers—the CEO wanted to make sure executives received the same dinner-time telemarketing phone calls that the company made to ordinary people.

Visiting the crime scene is: Peter Aceto, the CEO of Tangerine (formerly ING Direct), working in the call center and taking customer calls every day during his first year on the job. It's James Hereford, the CEO of Fairview Health Services in Minnesota, spending an hour with a different hospital unit every morning. It's Jim Lancaster, president of Lantech, walking through his whole company every morning for 60-90 minutes, visiting each department, observing the work, asking questions, and learning about the problems that his employees are grappling with.

When these leaders go and see, it's not as a tourist seeing a strange new land, or as a king visiting his serfs. They don't spend half their time in a conference room listening to some boilerplate presentation. And employees don't cover their butts by hiding problems and difficulties—they know that their leaders want to see the real conditions where the work is getting done.

As a result, when these leaders solve problems, they're able to leverage a deep understanding of the facts, buffering them from the temptation to jump to solutions.

Before you come up with a solution to a problem, go to the crime scene and see for yourself. Make sure you have the facts, not just the data.

HUMBLE INQUIRY

I don't know how Roger Smith spent his days, but I have to believe that during his nine-year tenure as CEO of GM, he must have walked through a factory at least a couple of times.

However, I'm not sure that he actually saw or learned anything.

He didn't see the skipped tool changes, the neglected quality checks, and who knows how many other clear symptoms of managerial malfeasance. Perhaps he missed them on his way to the separate, executive bathroom.

The second half of "go and see" is, well, *seeing*. If you're not going to open your eyes—and your ears, your mind, and your heart—you won't learn anything. You won't understand what's really happening. And you'll never be able to avoid jumping to conclusions.

When you go and see, you need to practice what management scholar Edgar Schein calls "humble inquiry." According to Schein, humble inquiry

> derives from an attitude of interest and curiosity. It implies a desire to build a relationship that will lead to more open communication. It also implies that one makes oneself vulnerable and, thereby, arouses positive helping behavior in the other person. Such an attitude is reflected in a variety of behaviors other than just the specific questions we ask. Sometimes we display through body language and silence a curiosity and level of interest that gets the other person talking even when we have said nothing.

Traditional hierarchical workplaces create unbalanced power dynamics that work against this kind of interaction. Nurses struggle to voice concerns about patient safety to surgeons. Software engineers have a hard time talking about coding problems to their project manager. First-year lawyers cringe at the thought of pushing back against the firm's practice leader. Young staff accountants are reluctant to question a partner on how they define "materiality" when they see shenanigans in the financial statements.

You only get real value out of going to the crime scene when you skip the royal tour and see how work is actually done. That requires you to consciously break down the hierarchical barriers in the organization.

Approach people with humility and ask questions that you don't already know the answer to so that you can learn and understand.

> Suspend judgment.
> Uncover the root cause.
> Take two steps back before
> you take one step forward.

That's how you avoid the impulse to jump to solutions.

YOU CAN BE YOUR OWN CRIME SCENE

You can "go and see" even if you work alone. You are your own crime scene, and you can approach your work in the same way.

Are you struggling to write a book, study a foreign language, or complete a project?

If you jump to conclusions, you'll probably create arbitrary goals and rules for yourself. For example, you might assume that you simply need a penalty to motivate yourself to work—so you vow not to have wine with dinner until you finish a chapter. Or you might assume that your house isn't the proper work environment, so you rent space in a co-working office. But those are the knee jerk solutions of the Jumper.

But if you go and see, you can start asking humble inquiry questions of yourself:

- What time of day do you work better?
- What's the correlation between how much sleep you get and how productive you are?
- How do you actually spend each hour of your workday?
- What pulls you away from writing—legitimate family commitments, or hours spent on Facebook? For that matter, why are you letting Facebook hijack your time and attention?

FRAME IT —PROPERLY

A problem well-stated is a problem half-solved.
—Charles Kettering, Head of Research,
General Motors

SOLVING A PROBLEM IS NOT A SINGLE, DISCRETE STEP. It's actually a process, and one that starts with a clear statement of what the problem actually is. Framing the problem properly is the first step on the road towards finding the right solution.

Problem statements are deceptively difficult to get right. For one thing, it's easy to mistake the symptoms for the underlying problem. For example, a child in Flint, MI might have behavioral issues in school and struggle with reading comprehension—but that's not the problem. Those are only symptoms. The real problem was the lead in the municipal water system.

And while you definitely have to deal with those symptoms, it's essential to address the underlying problem.

The Jumper inside you gravitates towards symptoms. They're easy to see and comparatively easy to address. It's the Analyst inside you that has the cognitive power to find the root cause of those symptoms, and to really fix the problem.

TIME, MONEY, AND PEOPLE ARE SELDOM THE REAL PROBLEM

How many times have you heard something like this (or said it yourself)? "The problem is that we don't have enough time to do…" Or, "The problem is that we need more money so that we can…" Or, "The problem is that we don't have enough people for…"

These sound like legitimate problems, right?

Not really.

These aren't problems. They're just evidence of lazy thinking. They're proof that you haven't thought deeply about the real problem.

The truth is you never have enough time. You never have enough money. And you never have enough people. There's not an organization on the planet—not Apple, not Amazon, not Google—where people are thinking, "Gee, I really wish corporate would cut my budget by 20%. I just don't know how to spend all this money I've got."

Oh, we're very clever. We would never explicitly acknowledge that we've jumped to a conclusion. But when you look closely, that's what those "problems" are. They're all solutions masquerading as problems. You can tell, because they're simply negations of your desired state.

The only possible answer to any of those so-called "problems" is having more time, spending more money, or hiring more people. Which are most often just lousy Band-Aids to the real underlying problems that you've got.

> What you need to do is spend time understanding the real problem first, before you go around spending money.

OPEN VISTAS VS. CUL-DE-SACS

A well-framed problem statement opens up avenues of discussion and options. A bad problem statement closes down alternatives and quickly sends you into a cul-de-sac of facile thinking.

Consider these two problem statements:

1. Our sales team needs more administrative support.
2. Our sales team spends 6 hours per week on low-value administrative tasks.

Although you hear this kind of framing often, notice that the first statement isn't really a problem at all. It's a solution. The only possible response to needing more administrative support is… to hire more administrative support.

What's the solution to the second problem statement? It's unclear—which is good!

The second problem statement pushes us to think analytically. The observable fact (six hours) rather than the implicit judgment (we need more admins) raises other questions that help us develop better solutions: why do they have six hours of administrative tasks in the first place? How can we make the tasks faster? Can we use a computer? Can we use checklists and templates to reduce the burden? Are they actually necessary? Can we eliminate some of them entirely?

If you see that your problem statement has only one solution, rethink it. Reframing the problem can help you avoid conclusion jumping.

UNDERSTAND THE GAP

Another example:

1. We need a better marketing campaign to promote our trail running series.

2. Only 35 people showed up for our last 10K road race, and we were expecting 200.

The first problem statement attacks the marketing efforts as inadequate. In this statement, there's already a conclusion—marketing stinks. Presumably that would entail finding a new agency, or hiring a new head of marketing, or spending more money. But how do we know that the marketing is the problem? Maybe there were other issues.

The second problem statement starts with an observable fact: 35 people, far less than the predicted number. With that information, we can start to ask deeper, thoughtful questions.

Why did we have so few people? What kind of support did our retail partner provide? What was the weather like that day? What promotional swag did we have at this event compared to previous events? Was the race course popular, or was it considered boring, or too hard? What else was going on in the community that day?

Answering these questions will lead to wisdom, and to better—and usually less expensive—solutions.

A final example, based on my friend's experience at the company where the senior leadership decided to buy $2 million worth of machines with six months wait time.

1. We don't have enough machines.

2. We don't have enough machine capacity.

The difference here is subtle: machines, versus machine **capacity**.

The leadership team probably thought to themselves, "We don't have enough presses to meet demand." That seems like a fair statement. And it was true. Up to a point.

But as in the earlier example, there's only one possible solution to the first problem statement: buy more machines.

The second problem statement creates space for alternative solutions. You could buy more machines, of course. But you could also run the machines for another shift. Or you could reduce the number of defects each machine produces, so you get more good parts out of each one. Or you could reduce the maintenance downtime for each machine, so you can get more productive hours each day out of each machine. Perhaps you could figure out a way to speed up the pressing process. You've got multiple solutions to consider.

The right wording can clarify—or obfuscate—the truth.

THE GOLDEN RULE

Writing a good problem statement is hard work.

Back to Einstein: "If I had an hour to solve a problem, I'd spend 55 minutes thinking about the problem and five minutes thinking about solutions."

The golden rule is to begin with observable facts, not opinions, judgments, or interpretations.

You want to describe what's actually happening. If you can answer questions like, "How much/How many/How long/How often," you're off to a good start—for example, "Only 12% of our prospects convert to customers." Or, "It takes 10 days to close our books each month." This kind of framing creates room for exploration and discovery.

Don't be afraid to iterate on your problem statement. As you think more deeply about the situation, you'll almost certainly modify your first version. That's okay. That's a sign that you understand more about the situation. This is the kind of data that will join with the facts you discover to lead you toward sounds decisions.

Once you have an acceptable problem statement, you can begin exploring why that problem exists. And you can begin to think backwards.

THINK
BACKWARDS

SINCE WE'RE TRYING TO AVOID THE TENDENCY TO LEAP TO CONCLUSIONS, it can be helpful to have a template that spurs the Analyst into action, rather than accepting our conclusion-jumping default. That's where the fishbone diagram comes in.

The fishbone diagram (also known as the Ishikawa diagram), was developed in the 1960s by Kaoru Ishikawa, a professor of engineering in Japan and an expert in quality control. It provides a clean, graphical method of identifying the potential factors causing a problem. It helps you understand how you got here—the point where the problem is severe enough that you need to fix it.

The factors are organized into logical groupings, which make the diagram look like the skeleton of a fish:

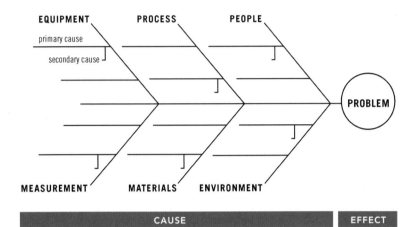

The classic fishbone diagram has six categories of factors, but this isn't a rule. You might have four categories or seven, and your categories might be different. A law firm, for example, probably won't need the Equipment category, while a software company might want to include a branch for Programming Language. The categories on the major "bones" of the skeleton are just a prompt to help you organize your thoughts. Obviously, the fishbone provides structure and organization for your analytical brainstorming. But more importantly, it encourages you to "think backwards"—to look for the issues that underlie the observable symptoms. Depending on the problem you're trying to solve, you might not need to identify secondary causes. Or you might need to dive down into tertiary causes. The individual fish bones are less important than the analysis they stimulate. The bones push you past the observable symptoms and encourage you to find root causes.

Here's an example of a fishbone analysis dealing with high employee turnover. Notice how the "Materials" branch has been replaced by something more relevant: External Environment.

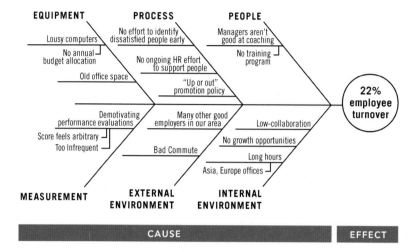

Here's a fishbone addressing a more personal issue—finishing a writing project. Of course, this would be relevant for any kind of project you're working on:

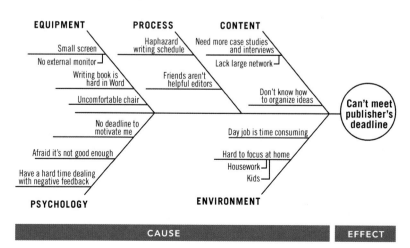

In this fishbone, "Measurement" is unimportant, but personal psychology is a real factor that needs to be addressed. And there's no bone for "People," since the subject is you. Remember, the fishbone is just a visual way to help you group your ideas into similar categories, but it's not necessary for thinking backwards. It's a tool, not a straitjacket. If it's intimidating, don't use it. You could accomplish the same thing in a table, where you put each category in a different column.

Here's what the employee turnover problem would look like in table format:

PROBLEM: 22% EMPLOYEE TURNOVER
CAUSES: (SEE BELOW)

EQUIPMENT	PROCESS	PEOPLE	MEASUREMENT	EXTERNAL ENVIRONMENT	INTERNAL ENVIRONMENT
Lousy computers ➡ No Annual Budget Allocation	No effort to identify dissatisfied people early	Managers aren't good at coaching ➡ No training program	Demotivating performance evaluations ➡ Arbitrary scores ➡ Infrequent	Many other good employers in our area	Low-collaboration
Old office space	No HR effort to support people				No growth opportunities
	Up or out promotion policy				Long hours ➡ Asia, Europe offices

FIVE
WHYS

5 WHY

**ASKING "WHY" REPEATEDLY IS A POWERFUL
WAY TO AVOID JUMPING TO CONCLUSIONS** and
implementing weak solutions. The concept is simple: ask "why"
multiple times before you settle on a conclusion. Now, it might
not take exactly five whys. It might only take three, or as many
as eleven, but eventually you'll get to the root cause.

In the case of the company president who wanted a smartphone
app to increase the sharing of leads, it probably would only have
taken one or two "whys?" to get to the root cause.

The key point to remember is not to accept the first conclusion you reach, which is generally a result of conclusion jumping.

In his book *Toyota Production System*, Taiichi Ohno details the most well-known example of how asking "why" gets you to the root cause:

1. **Why did the machine stop working?**
   Because the machine overloaded, blowing the fuse in the control panel.

2. **Why was there an overload?**
   Because there was insufficient lubrication to the spindle bearing.

3. **Why was there insufficient spindle bearing lubrication?**
   Because there was insufficient lubrication drawn up by the pump.

4. **Why was there insufficient lubrication draw from the pump?**
   Because the pump shaft was worn and rattling.

5. **Why was the pump shaft worn?**
   Because there was no strainer on the lubrication device inlet port, and small metal cutting chips entered the system causing damage.

Each question pushes you to a deeper understanding of the real problem. Stopping after any of the first four "whys?" would result in a Band-Aid that treats the symptom, rather than a solution that addresses the root cause. You could replace the fuse, add lubricant, get a new pump, or replace the pump shaft, but eventually your machine would once again break down.

Asking Five Whys is deceptively difficult. You might not go deep enough to find the true root cause. Or you can default to deductive reasoning and make assumptions, rather than getting facts from direct observation. Another risk is straying from the direct causal chain of events and getting bogged down in irrelevancies.

You also might need multiple rounds of Five Whys to deal with larger issues, because there's no single root cause in complex systems. For example, the 2008 financial crisis can't be explained—nor a solution found—with just one series of questions. We need to understand why rating agencies didn't fulfill their mission of providing accurate risk assessments of bonds; why banks were willing to underwrite so many risky mortgages; why people were motivated to take out mortgages that were too expensive for their income levels; why government regulation failed to protect the economy; etc.

FOUR STEPS TO AVOID JUMPING TO SOLUTIONS

I've recommending four steps to avoid jumping to solutions. If you follow them, you can put your internal Jumper on hold and activate the Analyst inside you:

1. Go and see
2. Frame the problem
3. Think Backwards
4. Five Whys

These four steps build on each other and work powerfully together to help you find effective and durable solutions to your problems.

When you *go and see* the work getting done at the crime scene, you get the facts.

When you observe the facts, you can *frame the problem* effectively, without relying on assumptions or potentially faulty interpretations of the data.

When you have a well-framed problem statement, you can *think backwards* and identify the issues that underlie the observable symptoms.

When you've identified the underlying issues, you can *ask why* those issues exist and find the root causes for the symptoms that you see.

But let's be clear: these four steps aren't actually a solution. Not at all.

These four steps will only provide you with a good problem statement—that is, a clearly defined problem—but not a solution. And although that's less immediately gratifying than a solution, it's a necessary precursor to finding something that really works.

PUTTING IT ALL TOGETHER

Here's an example of how I helped a recent client avoid the conclusion trap.

The company is a mid-sized manufacturer and distributer of camping and outdoor accessories. It does several million dollars per year in sales to Amazon.

While I was there, Amazon tightened its shipping policy, requiring its vendors to ship products in two days instead of three. The company was already struggling to deliver within the three day window, and now it was facing a 3% penalty on future orders if it couldn't figure out a way to process, pick, pack, and ship orders more quickly.

The leadership team first jumped to an obvious solution: hire more people in the warehouse. But of course, that would mean increasing expenses. We needed a better answer—and that meant following the four-step process:

Go and see: We literally followed an Amazon order from the time the customer service rep downloaded the electronic file to the time the boxes of products were sealed and ready for pickup. With first-hand observation, we could see numerous steps in the process where people had to wait unnecessarily to start their work, and other steps that could be completely eliminated. The facts and the data we gathered gave us a deeper understanding of the overall process.

Frame it: The knee-jerk description of the problem created by Amazon's policy change was, "We don't have enough people to process the Amazon orders in two days." Of course, the only solution to that kind of problem statement is to hire more people.

But with a better understanding of the overall process, the leadership team was able to reframe the problem: "Our current process is too slow to meet Amazon's requirements." Because this problem statement isn't a logical cul-de-sac, it provided opportunities for real improvement.

Think backwards: Once we framed the problem in a way that provided room to explore multiple solutions, we needed to provide a structure for our analysis. What were the causes of the slow process? Here's the fishbone we created:

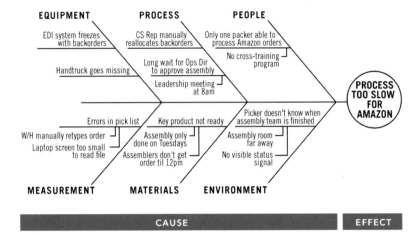

EQUIPMENT

EDI system freezes with backorders

Handtruck goes missing

PROCESS

CS Rep manually reallocates backorders

Long wait for Ops Dir to approve assembly

Leadership meeting at 8am

PEOPLE

Only one packer able to process Amazon orders

No cross-training program

PROCESS TOO SLOW FOR AMAZON

Errors in pick list

W/H manually retypes order

Laptop screen too small to read file

Key product not ready

Assembly only done on Tuesdays

Assemblers don't get order til 12pm

Picker doesn't know when assembly team is finished

Assembly room far away

No visible status signal

MEASUREMENT

MATERIALS

ENVIRONMENT

CAUSE

EFFECT

Five Whys: The fishbone gave us a structure that helped clarify the components of the problem. From there, asking "Why?" provided us with obvious—and inexpensive—countermeasures. For example, why did the warehouse manager retype the order for the picker? He was resorting the items on the pick list, because he thought that it would be helpful for the picker. In actuality, that step wasn't helpful at all and could be eliminated. Why was assembly of a key product only done on Tuesdays? Because the manufacturing schedule was established years before online ordering. When brick-and-mortar retailers ordered only a few times per season (rather than every Monday morning, like Amazon), it didn't matter what day of the week they assembled the product. But with weekly orders from Amazon, the team often had to wait for a day before the product was ready.

THE SOLUTION:

As with all complex problems, we needed to put multiple countermeasures in place. Each countermeasure saved time and allowed the Amazon order to flow through the system more quickly:

1. We changed the software allocation system so that anything out of stock was canceled, not back-ordered. This kept the EDI system from freezing, and allowed the customer service rep to process the order and deliver it to the warehouse more quickly.

2. The warehouse manager stopped retyping the pick list. This saved processing time and completely eliminated the data entry errors as well.

3. We spread product assembly out during the entire week, instead of batching it on Tuesdays. That ensured there would be more products available to fill the Amazon order.

4. The assembly team was given permission to begin work as soon as they received the order from customer service— they no longer waited for approval from the Director of Operations.

5. When the assembly team finished work, they brought the products to the packing area, instead of waiting for the picker to retrieve them.

6. We established a clear holding area for the warehouse hand trucks so that they wouldn't disappear.

When Amazon announced its policy change, the Director of Operations immediately jumped to the conclusion that he'd need to hire one or two more warehouse workers. As result of using this four step process, he was able to meet Amazon's tighter shipping window without hiring new staff, working overtime, or buying new warehouse equipment—even while increasing sales volume to Amazon. The company never had to pay a late shipping penalty. In fact, they're often ready to ship in only one day. The Director of Operations recently said to me, "Meeting Amazon shipping requirements is now boring. We don't even talk about it."

CAUTION: NO SILVER BULLETS

It would be great if all your problems could be fixed with a single silver bullet.

Unfortunately, life just isn't that simple—or at least, the problems you're dealing with aren't that simple. If they were, you'd have solved them by now.

In particular, the Five Whys and Thinking Backwards will usually reveal the need for a set of countermeasures to the problem. Because these tools help you understand a problem more deeply, you'll almost certainly find that the problem is multifactorial. As in the case of the camping goods company above, you'll need more than one "solution" to deal with it— not just a single magical, silver bullet.

As a result, just as you have to resist the temptation to jump to solutions, you'll have to overcome the urge to settle on a single countermeasure. A set of countermeasures is usually what's needed to deal with the thorny problems you face.

But don't be discouraged. Having multiple countermeasures increases the likelihood that you'll actually fix the problem for real.

RESIST THE SIREN SONG

As Matthew May says in his book, *The Elegant Solution*,

> *What appears to be the problem, isn't.*
> *What appears to be the solution, isn't.*

As human beings, we have a built-in tendency to jump to conclusions. We get seduced by what's easy. And our environment doesn't help. It's hard to resist the siren song—and the rewards—of speed over thoughtfulness.

This combination leads us to misunderstand the problems we face, inevitably leading to "solutions" that don't solve anything.

If you're careful, you can see the signposts warning you that you're jumping to conclusions. If you can't describe the problem as anything other than a lack of something—time, people, money, etc.—that's a sign you don't really understand the problem.

And reflexively reaching for new technology, reorganizing, or simply spending more money is a pretty good sign that you've jumped to a solution. Of course, you might actually need to do that sometimes—although not nearly as often as you might think.

But as Canby says in *The Phantom Tollbooth*, "[Jumping to conclusions is] such an easy trip to make that I've been here hundreds of times." I'm sure that you'll make that trip hundreds of times, too.

START THINKING NOW

I'm asking a lot of you.

I'm asking you to let go of what comes naturally. I'm asking you to say goodbye to what feels good. I'm asking you to break a habit that you've developed over years, if not decades.

I'm asking you to establish a new way of thinking, one in which you trust the cold "ambiguity of the why" over the warm comfort of the quick and easy answer.

I'm asking you to start building a new kind of muscle—a cognitive muscle. And just as you need to go to the gym everyday to develop physical muscles, you have to go to the mental gym everyday to exercise, develop, and strengthen this new way of thinking.

Unfortunately, I can't even promise that this approach will save you from making wrong decisions. In fact, I can guarantee that you'll **never** get all your decisions right. You'll also never get past the tendency to jump to conclusions.

That's okay. No one does. You're subject to the same human fallibilities as everyone else. It's part of the human condition.

But diligently following these four steps will keep you from your own worst tendencies. If you do so, you'll have a chance to make life better for yourself, for the people you manage, and for the people you care about.

Imagine not having to solve the same problems over and over again. Imagine a work life with less regret and frustration. Just for a moment imagine going home without complaining about yet another colossal waste of time, effort, and money at work. Doesn't that sound good?

That future isn't that far off.

Start now. Don't wait.